About the author

...g Laam Lei (方南理) is the Chinese ...or by his in-laws, who couldn't be ...ign devil barbarian in the family.

Having an income too small to gain acceptance among Hong Kong's white-skinned society and a nose too large to become assimilated among the Chinese, he inhabits a curious twilight zone inbetween these two sometimes harmonious, often conflicting worlds. So, while everybody else was out working for a living, the author had nothing better to do than to sit around sketching out this series of cartoons.

This book, then, is a collection of observations, insights, and all too many true-to-life incidents reflecting the annoyances and delights of life, people and language in Hong Kong.

About the words

This is not a dictionary. It isn't meant to teach you a thing. Call it a glossary, perhaps, of a few of the many things worth poking fun at in Hong Kong.

The words are Cantonese, the language of Hong Kong and of nearly every Chinatown around the world (Mandarin supremacists can just shut up!). As for pronunciation ... if you're not Chinese, forget it!! The problem with Cantonese is not that foreigners are patently unable to pronounce it, but that Chinese people *believe* that foreigners can't pronounce it (see page 31). If you must try, then ask a Chinese friend to read the words aloud to you.

About Hong Kong

A barren rock until 1841, now the most productive, densely-populated, hyperactive metropolis on earth, soon to be a barren rock again (see page 53). In the meantime, it's not a bad little colony ... er, territory ... I mean, Special Administrative Region to live in and laugh at!

Many of the cartoons in this book originally
appeared in the *Hongkong Standard.*

Originally published by Hongkong Standard.
Revised edition published by:

Hambalan Press
GPO Box 6086
Hong Kong

ISBN 962 7866 01 6
printed in Hong Kong

This revised edition was produced with the
assistance of a **Digital DECpc XL566 computer**
and a **Hewlett-Packard ScanJet IIc scanner**.

written and illustrated by

方 南 理
FONG LAAM LEI
(Larry Feign)

Chinese calligraphy by

Cathy Sau Yung Tsang-Feign,
M.A., M.S., M.F.C.C.

Special thanks to Cathy Tsang-Feign, Tsang Sau Mei, Tsang Shou Ping, Susan Noakes, John Keating, and Olivia Keith-Mitchell, for suggestions and assistance with this book.

The author is deeply grateful to Mr. Peter Yau, without whom this book would never have materialized.

To my darling wife Cathy, in spite of whose valiant and untiring efforts, I am still unable to put together a complete sentence in this impossible Cantonese dialect!

AIEEYAAA!

(excl.) The linchpin of Cantonese: a foreigner who pronounces this phrase with precision will gain new respect from local colleagues, especially if he/she habitually utters it every few seconds, anytime, anywhere, for any reason.

1

BA SI

(n.) Bus: popular amusement ride in Hong Kong, cheaper and more exciting than anything at Ocean Park. Offered in many variations, including:

THE KWUN TONG KRUNCHER

THE POKFULAM POUNCER

BAAT YUET SAP NG

(n.) 15th day of the 8th lunar month: the Moon Festival; also a euphemism for that part of the human anatomy which most resembles the moon. So beware if someone invites you over to "get the feel of" the occasion!

WHAT ARE YOU DOING FOR THE MOON FESTIVAL?

OH, I ALWAYS JUST SIT AROUND ON BAAT YUET SAP NG!

I KNOW!! I WAS TALKING ABOUT THE HOLIDAY!

BEI

(n.) Nose: yet another thing gwailo seem to need in gross excess, while Asians make do with more efficient compact models.

AIYEEYAAH!! WILL YOU QUIT PUSHING?!!

QUEUE HERE
TICKET HOLDERS
ONLY

SORRY. I DIDN'T REALISE.

BIU JE

(n.) Older female cousins other than the daughters of one's father's brothers... and if you can remember that, you're doing better than most Chinese!

SO, IF YOUR **YI MA**'S① HUSBAND'S **TONG DAAI LO**'S② WIFE'S **YI SAANG**'S③ **JAT JAI**④ IS MY HUSBAND'S **BIU SO**'S⑤ **SUK FOO**⑥, AND I'M A MONTH OLDER, THAT MAKES ME YOUR **TONG GA JE**⑦, RIGHT?

NO, STUPID! I'M NOT YOUR **SOH TONG SAI LO**⑧! ... I'M YOUR **BIU DAI**⑨, SO YOU'RE MY **BIU JE!**

NG FAMILY REUNION

PARTY

1) 姨媽 Mother's elder sister
2) 堂大佬 Father's brother's son (older)
3) 姨甥 Sister's son
4) 姪仔 Brother's son
5) 表嫂 Mother's sister's son's wife (older)
6) 叔父 Father's younger brother
7) 堂家姐 Father's brother's daughter (older)
8) 疏堂細佬 Father's brother's son (younger)
9) 表弟 Mother's sister's son (younger)

5

報紙

BO JI

(n.) Newspaper. Few of the 66 dailies published in Hong Kong ever contain any actual news, since no one reads the paper for that anyway.

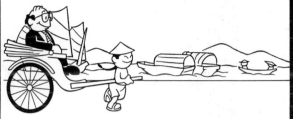

CHA

(n.) Tea. In theory, nearly the only thing the English and the Chinese have in common. But certainly not in practice...

WAITER... MORE SUGAR, PLEASE!

CHAU DAU F[1]O

(n.) Bean curd fermented in an extract from the unwashed socks of six football teams. Traditionally used to ward off vampires and other vermin.

CHEONG SAM

(n.) Alluring figure-hugging gown worn by almond-eyed temptresses on the covers of racy novels. Today you're as likely to see one worn in public as you are to see a junk with actual sails.

THE GOOD OLD DAYS

TODAY

CHEUNG

(n.) Window: openings placed in buildings to allow air in and garbage out.

SIGH... CAN'T THEY DO SOMETHING ABOUT PEOPLE TOSSING RUBBISH OUT THEIR WINDOWS??

THEY HAVE!

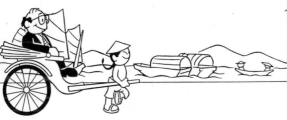

CHI SIN

(n./adj) Crossed wires; more commonly means "crazy". The former happens so often with Hong Kong telephones, it'll turn you into the latter!

CHIN

(n.) Money: of course it's more important than love, since, over time, romantic interest wanes, but capital interest gains.

SIGH... ALL WE EVER TALK ABOUT ANYMORE IS MONEY! WHAT EVER HAPPENED TO ALL THOSE ROMANTIC THINGS YOU USED TO TELL ME?

YOUR EYES ARE AS BLUE AS $50 BILLS... YOUR LIPS ARE AS PINK AS $100 BILLS... YOUR HAIR IS AS GOLDEN AS $1000 BILLS...

STOCKS

TAX SHELTERS

CHING GIT

(adj.) Clean; "Everybody loves a clean Hong Kong," we're told ...though they never mention Kowloon or the Harbour, since that would be asking too much!

CHOI

(n.) Vegetables: something Chinese would never eat raw and never overcook, unlike westerners, who eat them no other way.

AHH! A PERFECT SALAD! THREE TYPES OF LETTUCE, SPINACH, CELERY, PEPPERS, CARROTS, CHIVES, TOMATOES, ONIONS, OLIVES, MUSHROOMS, ANCHOVIES, CHEESE, PARSLEY, DILL, TARRAGON, OIL AND VINEGAR... LET'S SEE, HAVE I FORGOTTEN ANYTHING?

YES!

...TO COOK IT!

SEA SALT

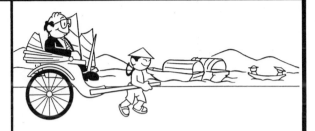

CHUEN FOO GE

(n.) Pager: item carried into cinemas, plays, concerts, churches and restaurants as an audible reminder to the rest of the world of just how important you are.

CHILDHOOD   ADOLESCENCE   ADULTHOOD

CHUNG LEUNG

(v.) Shower: yet another point of contention between Orientals and Occidentals.

AHH, THERE'S NOTHING LIKE A SHOWER IN THE MORNING TO WAKE ME UP AND GET ME GOING FOR THE DAY!

AHH, THERE'S NOTHING LIKE A SHOWER IN THE EVENING TO RELAX ME AND HELP ME FALL ASLEEP!

DA

(v.) Hit, punch, beat. Also means (n.) dozen. (don't ask me what the heck the connection is!)

17

DA FUNG

(n.) Typhoon: unscheduled public holidays declared at the whim of the Royal Observatory.

ROYAL OBSERVATORY

HUH??!! WHAT DO YOU MEAN YOUR MOTHER'S FLYING IN FROM MALAYSIA TONIGHT?!!

...AND WE'VE HAD A SUDDEN ANNOUNCEMENT THAT THE ROYAL OBSERVATORY HAS RAISED THE SIGNAL #8. ALL PUBLIC SERVICES, INCLUDING THE AIRPORT, ARE CLOSED...

DAAI DAAM

(n.) "Big bladder": the Chinese equivalent of "a lot of guts"... though in either language it's a mystery how courage became associated with a swollen urinary or digestive tract!

SUPERHEROES of EAST & WEST

LOT-A-GUTS MAN

BIG BLADDER BOY

DAAN

(n.) The humble egg; though in Hong Kong, even something as ordinary as an egg is never quite that simple...

TWO EGGS, OVER EASY!

YES, SIR. WILL THOSE BE PIGEON, DUCK, QUAIL, CHICKEN, GOOSE, HUMMINGBIRD, PARTRIDGE, PELICAN, FLAMINGO, MONGOOSE, ALLIGATOR...

DAK HAAN

(adj.) To have free time: condition attributable exclusively to expatriate wives.

21

DEI TO

(n.) Map: colourful banner issued to visitors by the Tourist Association as a service to jade hawkers, pickpockets and Indian tailors.

FOR HEAVEN'S SAKE, HAROLD! PUT AWAY THOSE STUPID MAPS ALREADY!!

YOU WANT PEOPLE TO THINK WE'RE **TOURISTS** OR SOMETHING?!

DIK SI

(n.) Taxi: the most terrifying form of transportation in Hong Kong — I don't mean the drivers, I mean the meters!

STOP! STOP! FOR GOD'S SAKE, STOP!!

WHAT??! BUT WE'RE IN THE MIDDLE OF THE HARBOUR TUNNEL!

TAXI 的士

I'M NOT TALKING TO YOU! I'M TALKING TO THE METER!

CLICK!

29 40

DIM SUM

(n.) "A little bit of heart"... or liver or intestine or gall bladder, or whatever else can be rolled up and steamed or fried.

DIN TAI

(n.) Lift/elevator : 30 or so square feet of the area you couldn't account for when your "800 square foot" flat turned out to be smaller than advertised.

YOU USE THE LIFTS, HALLWAY, FOYER, FLOWER BASIN, RUBBISH ROOM, AND STAIRWAY, RIGHT? ADD THEM TOGETHER, YOU GOT 1500 SQUARE FEET, LIKE I SAID!

DUEN NG JIT

(n.) Dragon Boat Festival: annual commemoration of the drowning suicide of Wat Yuen (屈原) in protest of government wrongdoing. This festival will be prohibited after 1997, since obviously there will be no government wrongdoing.

MIND IF WE JOIN IN?

CCCP

DUK SUE

(v.) Study; there must be enormous competition in the UHK Zoology Department, otherwise why do you see practically everyone in Hong Kong spending every spare minute studying horses?

LOOK AT HIM! WASTING ALL DAY WITH THOSE STUPID NUMBERS! WHY CAN'T YOU DO SOMETHING PRACTICAL LIKE YOUR BROTHER?!

LEAVE HIM ALONE, MOM! HE'LL GROW OUT OF IT!

RACING

RACE 1 RACE 2

RACING

CHEMISTRY

CALCULUS

ENGINEERING

DESIGN

PHYSICS

FAAI JI

(n.) Chopsticks: don't bother trying to use them — your Chinese dinner companions will only be disappointed if you can.

CAN YOU USE CHOPSTICKS?

ER...NO. WHY DON'T YOU COME UP TO MY PLACE AND SHOW ME WHERE TO PUT MY FINGERS...!

帆船

FAAN SUEN

(n.) Junk: form of false advertising used by the Tourist Association to lure unwary visitors, who also expect to see a Hong Kong peopled by Suzie Wongs and opium-smoking rickshaw coolies all eating in floating restaurants.

I THOUGHT HONG KONG'S HARBOUR WAS FULL OF JUNKS!

IT IS!

FAAT GWOON

(n.) Court judge: man who wears a long blonde wig, frilly dress and pantyhose in public and sends other men to prison for doing the same thing.

BEFORE I PASS SENTENCE, THE DEFENDANT WILL PLEASE INFORM THE COURT...

WHO'S YOUR TAILOR?

FAAT YAM

(n.) Pronunciation: a lost cause for foreigners attempting Cantonese. If, by sheer accident, you do say it right, people will only assume you were actually mispronouncing something else!

SAI SAU GAAN HAI BIN DO AH?✳

✳ 洗手間喺邊度呀?
Where's the rest room?

ER... SAAAI SAAAU GAAAAAN HAAAAI BIIIIN DOOOOOH AAAAAAAHH...?

S-S-SAAIII S-S-SAAAUUU G-G-G-G-G—

YAAAAAA

SOUNDED LIKE THE FOREIGNER WAS ASKING WHERE'S A REST ROOM!

I WONDER WHAT HE WAS REALLY TRYING TO SAY?

FAN YAN

(n.) Marriage: for many men, it's not so much a union with one woman as it is the enforced separation from all the others.

SOB!! MARRIED ONLY TWO YEARS AND ALREADY YOU'RE STARTING TO SPEND TIME WITH ANOTHER WOMAN!

WHO ARE YOU TALKING ABOUT?

YOUR WIFE!

GA

(n.) Family: the people who will always accept you just the way you are and never hesitate to tell you how you should be.

FRED, THIS IS YOUR MOTHER. DID YOU SEND YOUR SISTER A BIRTHDAY CARD?

ER...AH... SIGH!...I'LL SEND ONE TODAY...

1

WANDA, THIS IS YOUR MOTHER. IF YOU GET A CARD FROM YOUR BROTHER, IT WOULD BE NICE IF YOU'D CALL HIM TO SAY THANKYOU!

OH... ALRIGHT...

2

FRED? MOTHER AGAIN. IF YOUR SISTER CALLS TO THANK YOU FOR THE CARD, PLEASE TRY TO SAY SOMETHING NICE ABOUT HER HUSBAND.

3

SIGH... IT'S SO NICE TO HAVE A CLOSE FAMILY WHO CARE ABOUT EACH OTHER!

4

GAAT JAAT

(n.) Cockroach: omnipresent freeloaders on Kowloon buses. If only they would pay their fares, perhaps KMB could finally afford to have the buses cleaned!

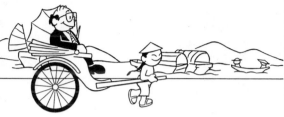

GAAU DOI

(n.) Sea organisms which inhabit Hong Kong coastal areas by the millions. Commonly termed "plastic bags", they are often seen stuffed with vegetables or clothing and carried around on the street.

35

GAN

(n.) Catty: Chinese unit of weight roughly equal to 1¼ pounds. Unless, of course, you're a gwai lo, in which case the catty of onions you just paid for is more likely around 8 ounces.

GAU LUNG

(n.) Kowloon: taken in 1860 "in perpetuity" by the British when they realised how much better the shopping was than on Hong Kong island.

AT HOME WITH GOVERNOR AND MRS. ROBINSON, MARCH 1860...

OH, DEAR, HERKY! THE STRUANS ARE COMING FOR TEA! WHERE AM I GOING TO GET PENINSULA CHOCOLATES TO SERVE THIS TIME OF NIGHT??

GET ME GENERAL STRAUBENZEE!... STRAUBY? QUICK! ANNEX KOWLOON!!

GOH SING

(n.) Singer: mannequin with nice teeth whose popularity and inflated sense of self-importance are in inverse ratio to their originality and ability to sing.

WHY DO YOU IDOLIZE THIS IDIOT?? HE'S GOT NO VOICE, NO PERSONALITY, NO RHYTHM, SINGS THE SAME SYRUPY MUSH AS EVERYONE ELSE... WHY DON'T THEY PUT SOMEONE WITH **TALENT** ON FOR A CHANGE??!

WHAT? AND MAKE ALL THE OTHER STARS LOSE FACE??

OH OH OH CALOR!

SUPER STARS OF HONG KONG

GONG

(n.) Harbour : world-famous Victoria Harbour yearly attracts thousands of ships, millions of tourists, 37 billion tons of raw sewage, plastic bags and soda pop cans, and maybe even one or two fish; perhaps the most beautiful septic tank on earth!

BREATHTAKING, ISN'T IT?

GORGEOUS.

I WASN'T TALKING ABOUT THE VIEW!

GONG GA

(v.) Bargain: the art of paying only 10% more than you should have for something that costs twice as much and is worth 30% less than the thing you wanted to buy in the first place.

GEE, IF THINGS ARE THAT BAD, FORGET I ASKED YOU TO KNOCK ANOTHER $100 OFF THE PRICE!!

GUNG CHAAN JUE YI

(n.) Communism: utopian doctrine under which the majority of people labour 14 hours a day knee-deep in water buffalo dung while petty do-nothing officials cruise around in shiny BMWs ...and you thought China and Hong Kong had different systems?

SOME OF US ARE MORE EQUAL THAN OTHERS!

GUNG HEI FAAT CHOI

(excl.) Chinese New Year greeting, meaning: "Congratulations, get rich!"...though this never actually happens to anyone at New Year, except hair stylists and children's clothing dealers.

GUNG MAN KUEN

(n.) Citizenship; the question of post-1997 citizenship has already been settled: if present trends continue, by then everyone will be Canadian!

...TO HAVE AND TO HOLD, UNTIL CITIZENSHIP DO YOU PART...

WINK!

APPLICATION FOR CITIZENSHIP

APPLICATION FOR CITIZENSHIP

APPLICATION FOR CITIZENSHIP

VANCOUVER

GUNG YAI

(n.) Amah: doctors, professors and nuclear physicists from the Philippines who come here because they can earn five times as much money scouring toilets and spending all day waiting on little runny-nosed brats.

HAVEN'T YOU FINISHED MY BIOLOGY HOMEWORK YET?!! **YOU LAZY WENCH!!** YOU EXPECT ME TO WAIT, ALL NIGHT FOR YOU TO BRUSH MY TEETH??!!

EVENING, ANITA! TOMMY MUST BE IN BED...? O.K., WE WON'T DISTURB HIM!

GWAI JIT

(n.) Season: changes in weather created by God as a service to the fashion industry.

HONG KONG

香 港

ALL-SEASON PARADISE

RAINY SEASON

MELT AND MILDEW

MORE MILDEW

STILL MORE MILDEW

TYPHOON SEASON

TWO WEEKS IN OCTOBER

AAAH!

FREEZIN' SEASON

GWAI LO

(n.) Literally translates as "ghost chap" and not "white uncivilized hairy-faced heathen barbarian devil" as is commonly believed.

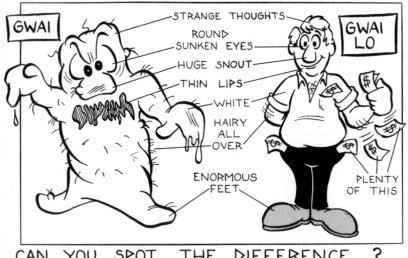

GWAI

STRANGE THOUGHTS

ROUND SUNKEN EYES

HUGE SNOUT

THIN LIPS

WHITE

HAIRY ALL OVER

ENORMOUS FEET

GWAI LO

$

PLENTY OF THIS

CAN YOU SPOT THE DIFFERENCE...?

GWOK SUT

(n.) Chinese martial arts: everybody's heard of Kung Fu and T'ai Chi, but for a true display of fighting skill, dexterity and stamina, just go into any MTR station on a weekday morning!

① ② ③ ④

PARDON ME, IS THIS SEAT TAKEN?

GWONG TAU

(n./adj.) Bald head; Chinese aren't as vain as westerners when it comes to baldness—they think of it not as losing hair but as gaining face!

ANOTHER FALLEN HAIR! *SIGH*... I'LL BE BALD BEFORE I'M 40!

THERE'S A CHINESE SAYING THAT 9 OUT OF 10 BALD MEN ARE RICH!

OH YEAH? THEN THIS PLACE MAKES THE PEAK SEEM LIKE A SQUATTER AREA IN COMPARISON!

PO LIN MONASTERY 寶蓮寺

GWOO LO YUK

(n.) Sweet-and-sour pork.
Often jokingly called GWAI LO
YUK (鬼佬肉)... or is it really meant as a joke?

NOT THAT ONE!
I WANT ONE WITH
BETTER TASTE!!

HA HA HA HA HA

(excl.) No, nothing funny has just been said; it's just the Chinese way of saying: "I see. Yes. Quite."

I THINK I LOOK SMASHING IN A CHEONG SAM, DON'T YOU AGREE?

HA HA HA HA HA!

I'LL NEVER UNDERSTAND THESE STUPID BARBARIANS!!

HAK YAN JANG

(n.) Negro monk; but actually means "disgusting bum". This is Chinese rhyming slang (rhymes with HAT YAN JANG 乞人憎: "detestable beggar") and not an overt racial slur... though try explaining that in Harlem, Brixton, or Kampala...!

51

HEI SAN

(v.) Wake up: what most people do at 7:00 a.m., and, if they're in government, again at 4:45 p.m..

52

HEUNG GONG

(n.) Hong Kong: tiny tropical colony called by Chairman Mao a "pimple on the bum of China"... though it's the British government that's done most of the squeezing.

1 JULY 1997

WE'RE RETURNING IT JUST AS WE FOUND IT!

HING GUNG

(n.)The ability to fly: all Chinese have this ability, as evidenced on TV — so why don't more people use it and beat the crowds on the MTR??

SUNG DYNASTY RUSH HOUR

HING SUNG

(v.) Relax: the way some people in Hong Kong relax sure makes it hard for others to relax!

好

HO

(adj./adv.) Good/well; also means very... and you probably thought all those "ho ho's" from your colleagues were just their laughing off the idea every time you threaten to quit your job!

1. NEI HO MA? *

HO.

2.

3. *I AM!* HO MISERABLE. HO EXHAUSTED. HO SICK OF MY JOB. HO FED UP WITH MY WIFE. HO DISGUSTED WITH MY KIDS...

BUT YOU DON'T LOOK "HO"!

* 你好嗎？
HOW ARE YOU?

HOK

(v.) Learn; the reason foreigners can't learn Cantonese is not that gwailo are stupid or that Cantonese is difficult, but because no one will let them learn it!

YAU MO CHAANG JAP?*

YES, SIR, RIGHT HERE!

* 有冇橙汁
Do you have orange juice?

GEI DO CHIN?*

FOUR DOLLARS!

* 幾多錢
How much is it?

M GOI!!*

THANK YOU!!

* 唔該
Thank you.

JERK!! CAN'T HE SEE I SPEAK CANTONESE?!!

JERK!! CAN'T HE SEE I SPEAK ENGLISH?!!

HUNG

(adj.) Empty: as in the seat next to yours in a crowded bus or fast food restaurant, if you're gwailo.

58

JAAN SEUNG

(v.) Compliment; a westerner finds it rude when a compliment is rejected, while a Chinese finds it arrogant when one is accepted... no wonder neither side ever has anything nice to say about the other!

JAAT GEUK

(v./n.) Foot binding: though outlawed in 1911, this archaic practice is making a comeback among expats, for whom it's the only hope in getting shoes to fit them in Hong Kong!

JAAU WOON DIM

(n.) Money Changer : company
in the business of changing
your money... into theirs.

61

JAM GAU

(n.) Acupuncture: a treatment involving needles being stuck all over your body, which doesn't hurt at all... until you get stuck with the bill!

JAU LAU

(n.) Chinese restaurant; if McDonald's and Wendy's are the products of crass American cultural imperialism, how do you explain the millions of Chinese restaurants that proliferate in nearly every city, town and village on earth?

LITTLE-KNOWN FACT #437:
A FAMOUS PLAY BY SHAKESPEARE WAS BASED ON HIS EXPERIENCES IN A CHINESE RESTAURANT...

Wong's CHOPPE SUEY
YE OLDE SPECIAL
GINGER CHICK BEAN CURD
BAMBOO BAMBBO SHOOTS

HMMMM... TWO B'S OR NOT TWO B'S, THAT IS THE QUESTION...

FORSOOTH! THAT GIVETH ME AN IDEA!

JE

(n.) Umbrella: device for the removal of eyeballs from anyone over 5 feet tall.

THAT'S A CLEVER WAY TO PROTECT YOURSELF FROM THE RAIN!

IT'S NOT THE RAIN I'M WORRIED ABOUT!!

借借

JE JE

(excl.) "Excuse me!": 2 words heard only from newcomers to Hong Kong, who need to excuse themselves for being so naïve as to think anyone will heed such a request.

① DING!

②

③ DOESN'T ANYBODY SAY "EXCUSE ME" ANYMORE?!

④ 'SCUSE ME EXCUSE ME JE JE EXCUSE ME JE JE

JI

(n.) Paper: first invented in China 105 A.D.. First crumpled up and dumped on the ground 106 A.D. at Wong Tai Sin, where it hasn't been swept up since.

THE INVENTION OF PAPER...

WHAT'S IT FOR?

MARK SIX
3 4 5 6 7 8
11 12 13 14 15
17 20 21 22

JIK MAN DEI

(n.) Colony: what Hong Kong is and always will be, whether the masters are from the United or Middle Kingdom.

THAT HOUSE ON THE PEAK IS MINE!

NO WAY! YOU ALREADY GET THOSE FLATS IN STANLEY!!

KOWLOON TONG?? I'LL RESIGN IF THEY PUT ME THERE!!

MY WIFE DEMANDS A PLACE WITH TENNIS COURTS AND SAUNA!

HOW'S THE T.V. RECEPTION IN SHEKO?

WE'LL CHANGE RACE DAYS TO MONDAYS!

BUT THAT'S "DYNASTY" NIGHT!

WHERE YOU GOING TO KEEP YOUR YACHT?

THE POLITBURO DISCUSSES THE FUTURE OF THE HONG KONG S.A.R.

JIP DOI YUEN

(n.) Receptionist: person who is paid to never know the whereabouts of the boss or the time of his return; better known as a **de**ceptionist.

I'D LIKE TO SPEAK TO MR. NG!

SORRY, MAYBE YOU CALL LATER!

LATER...

MR. NG, PLEASE!

SORRY, MAYBE YOU CALL LATER!

LATEST...

IS MR. NG BACK YET??

SORRY, MAYBE YOU CALL LATER!

ANY CALLS YET, CHERIE?

SORRY, MAYBE YOU ASK LATER!

RING!

MR. NG, PLEASE!!

CLICK! SORRY, MAYBE YOU CALL LATER!

CLICK!

POP STARS

JUET MONG

(adj.) Hopeless: it's not the awful mess left in Statue Square on Sundays that makes one feel hopeless... it's that this comes after 100,000 professional housecleaners spent the day there!

JUK

(n.) Congee: last night's leftover rice reboiled into a lumpy paste with scraps of meat dropped in; a breakfast so lacking in texture and flavour that it could have been invented by the English.

JUN LEUNG

(v.) That nauseatingly ubiquitous response: "I try my best!", which is Hongkongese for: "I'll do nothing of the sort!"

JUNG GWOK

(n.) China: expansionist empire which seeks "reunification" with any place that happens to have a Chinese population.

JUNG MAN

(n.) Chinese: literally means "language of the nation around which the rest of the world revolves"... and you always thought that was English!

STOP HERE, PLEASE! I SAID STOP, PLEASE!

PUBLIC LIGHT BUS

HELLO? STOP, I SAID! STOP, WOULD YOU?! **I SAID STOP!!**

STOP, DAMN IT!! STOP!! STOP! STOP! YAAAAA!!!

I THOUGHT THEY ALL UNDERSTAND ENGLISH!

WELL, SOME PEOPLE ARE TOO STUPID TO LEARN A FEW SIMPLE WORDS IN ANOTHER LANGUAGE!

KAU TAU

(v.) "Kowtow": now reduced to a symbolic gesture of tapping one's finger when tea is poured, the ancient custom of "striking the head" on the ground is otherwise extinct, except in the minds of wishful-thinking foreigners.

KOWTOW!

LAAP SAAP TUNG

(n.) Rubbish bin: decorative orange fixtures placed at intervals along Hong Kong pavements and used chiefly as spittoons.

LAI SI

(n.) Money handed out in little red envelopes: annual tariff extorted by children, employees, and apartment building security guards.

LAI YI

(n.) Courtesy: archaic term that disappeared from usage in Hong Kong decades ago and hasn't been heard of since.

LEI DO

(n.) Outer islands: former havens of peace and tranquility, now havens for plastic bags, industrial waste, chicken bones and ghetto blaster boom boxes.

LEUNG CHA

(n.) Chinese herbal medicine: potions which cure any illness by tasting so incredibly vile that your body instantly heals itself just to avoid a 2nd dose.

LOK GWOON

(n.) Optimist: one who says that Hong Kong's future after 1997 is full of nothing but promise; whereas a pessimist is one who says the same thing.

SO, HOW DO YOU LIKE IT NOW THAT HONG KONG IS PART OF CHINA?

CAN'T COMPLAIN!

I KNOW!

South China Evening Mail
10 rmb 13 JUNE 1998

NEW 5-YEAR PLAN

WAR IS PEACE

JAYWALKER EXECUTED

South China Evening Mail
13 JUNE 1998
EVERYTHING IS WONDERFUL SAY GOVT EXPERTS

PEOPLE DEMAND END TO DEMOCRACY

LUNG

(n.) Dragon; also means queue, aptly enough, since in Hong Kong both are mythical phenomena.

MA JEUK

(n.) Most popular noise-making activity in Hong Kong, now that firecrackers are banned.

HOW TO PLAY MA JEUK (MAH JONG)

① DISTRIBUTE AMMUNITION

② ERECT FORTIFICATIONS

③ EXCHANGE MONEY

④ LET THE BATTLE BEGIN!

MAAI YE

(v.) To shop: the be-all and end-all of culture in Hong Kong.

WHERE SHALL WE GO TONIGHT — THE THEATRE, A CONCERT, OR A GALLERY EXHIBITION?

WHERE WE GOING TONIGHT — TO SHOP FOR CLOTHES, FURNITURE, OR DISHES?

LONDON

HONG KONG

MIN

(n.) Face: something Asians are always afraid of losing ... though with the faces many people put on display, the loss would be an improvement.

BUT WHY ARE YOU PUNISHING HIM? HE GOT STRAIGHT 100'S ON HIS SCHOOL REPORT!

HE MADE HIS SISTER LOSE FACE!

WHACK!

MO

(v.) To not have: the automatic conditioned response of Hong Kong salesclerks to any request that would require either thought or movement.

YAU MO* CLA—

MO.

※ 有冇 Do you have

—ssical music... YAU MO J; MO.

—azz...DO YOU HAVE **ANY**THING BESIDES

MO.

Sigh!...THIS IS THE 18th SHOP IN A ROW THAT HAS NOTHING I'M LOOKING FOR!!

NGAAM NGAAM HO

(adj.) Perfect fit/just perfect; for a breath of fresh optimism in Hong Kong, go into any clothing or shoe store, where you'll always hear that everything is just perfect!

銀
行

NGAN HONG

(n.) Bank: temples of worship to the indigenous religion of Hong Kong.

NGOH

(pron.) I/me: the only person who exists in this city-state of 5½ million people.

NGOI

(v./n.) Love: emotion associated with blindness, falling, burning, madness, bewitchery, addiction and heart disorders, and which should therefore be prohibited.

PA SAAN

(v.) To hike: a common weekend diversion... except in Hong Kong, where the only hiking you'll ever notice is that of vegetable prices during holidays or typhoons.

HIKING
EUROPEAN
STYLE

SALE

HIKING
HONG KONG
STYLE

PAAI DUI

(v.) Queue: wait in line without pushing or shoving; another weird barbaric foreign custom.

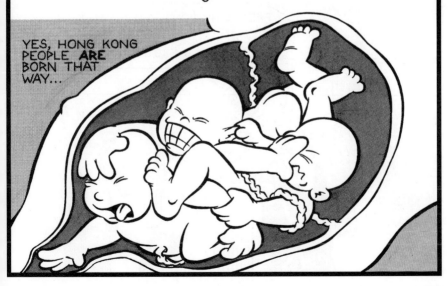

YES, HONG KONG PEOPLE **ARE** BORN THAT WAY...

朋友

PANG YAU

(n.) Friend: what others call you if you can refer them some business; otherwise they don't call you at all!

FRED, WHY DON'T YOU GO TALK TO BILL INSGATE. YOU TWO HAVE A LOT IN COMMON — YOU EACH MAKE UNDER $80,000 A MONTH!

SAAM

(n.) Three: number of times you have to ask before a Chinese person will admit what you suspected in the first place.

SAI GAAI

(n.) The world: vast area somewhere beyond Tsuen Wan where Hong Kong products disappear to and gwailo mysteriously come from.

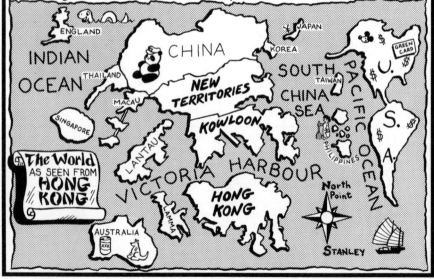

SAI LO

(n.) Children: diminutive creatures utilized solely to hold up traffic on the pavement.

SAI YAN

(n.) Westerner ; synonym
for "walking bank vault."

SAN GAAI

(n.) New Territories : area leased to the British, who should thank God that the Chinese lessors of 1898 bore no resemblance to present-day Hong Kong landlords.

FIRST AND LAST DECADES' RENT UP FRONT, TWO DECADES AS SECURITY DEPOSIT, AGENT'S FEE OF THREE DECADES' RENT, MANAGEMENT FEE, NO PETS, NO SUBLETTING, NO UNAUTHORISED STRUCTURES, NO MANUFACTURING ON THE PREMISES, NOT RESPONSIBLE FOR TYPHOON DAMAGE....

FOR RENT ...cheap!

SAP FAN

(adv.) Completely; also means ten minutes, which is about how long it takes for most foreigners to completely give up trying to learn Cantonese.

I LOVE YOU ALWAYS AND FOREVER, UNTIL THE END OF TIME!

I LOVE YOU TEN MINUTES!

WHAT DID I SAY WRONG??!

SAU YAM GEI

(n.) Radio. In bilingual Hong Kong, we are lucky to have a choice between Cantonese stations, featuring incessant mind-numbing witless chatter occasionally interrupted by the ten songs the stations possess; or English stations, which feature the same thing in reverse.

SEI

(n./adj.) Four: the unluckiest number of all, since it sounds like SEI (死), a morbid curse; could this explain why Chinese like to avoid for-eigners?

OPERATOR, CAN YOU GIVE ME THE NUMBER FOR BRIGHTER WONDERFUL LUCKY GOLDEN FORTUNATE SUCCESS CO., LTD.?

SEI SEI SEI SEI SEI SEI SEI.

SAME TO YOU !!!

SLAM!

SI

(n.) Silk: material made from the saliva of baby moths. If a similar product could be created from human spittle, Hong Kong would be the world capital of the industry!

MRS. SILKWORM SENDS BOBBY OFF TO SCHOOL

SI JONG

(n.) Fashion: standards of bad taste devised so that people with no taste know what to wear.

SIK

(v.) Eat: the saying goes that "Chinese will eat anything with its back facing heaven"... which could be why you never see anyone bowing at Chinese banquets!

WAITER, THERE'S A FLY IN MY SOUP!!

SORRY, SIR. THE LIZARD MUST HAVE COUGHED IT UP!

SIK YIN

(v.) To smoke tobacco: sooty, toxic habit which, curiously, is considered acceptable to do in public, while less harmful and obtrusive habits aren't.

SING JOH HOK

(n.) Astrology: people with uncertainties about the future used to consult the stars; these days they just get foreign passports.

105

SUEN GUI

(n.) Election: of course we'll still have them after 1997...

Beijing's policy on Hong Kong's future has always been the embodiment of hypocri— I mean, democracy!

SUEN MEI

(n.) Beauty contest: anyone who places 28th runner-up or above in any of these weekly summer events automatically becomes a "singer" or "actress", with no credentials other than nice bone structure...which is at least better than can be said for some Legco members!

WHAT IF OUR POLITICIANS WERE SELECTED THE WAY OUR "ACTRESSES" ARE...

AND THE **MISS TOADY** AWARD GOES TO...

LEGCO 37 Pageant

TAU SO

(v.) Complain: something few people in Hong Kong will do, since even fewer people will listen.

THIS RECORD I BOUGHT HERE YESTERDAY IS BADLY WARPED!

VERY SORRY, SIR.

WELL...???

WELL WHAT? I APOLOGISED, DIDN'T I?

TIN CHOI

(n.) Talent: trite overused word employed by disc jockeys and entertainment reviewers to describe anyone whose main talent is making a lot of money off the talents of others.

① ENGLISH (OR JAPANESE) HIT SONG APPEARS ON RADIO.

Feelings
WO WO WO...

② TRANSLATOR RENDERS INTO CANTONESE.

要錢唔
要面!
要金唔
要心!!

③ ARRANGER TRAN-SCRIBES SCORE.

④ MUSICIANS PERFORM SCORE.

⑤ PRETTY-BOY (OR -GIRL) WITH CUTE NOSE AND WHITE TEETH PROPPED UP AT MICROPHONE.

⑥ PRODUCER EDITS, RE-MIXES AND ENHANCES RECORDING

⑦ DESIGNER CREATES COVER.

⑧ WHO GETS THE CREDIT?

THAT LEON LAI IS SO TALENTED!!

TIN GAI

(n.) Frog: lumpy green creature which lives in putrid slime, eats flies and other vermin, and is proof that Chinese are not such picky eaters as they claim!

TIN HEI

(n.) Weather; strange, isn't it, that our TV weather reports are sponsored by watches, since watches are supposed to be accurate!

THE WEATHER REPORT IS BROUGHT TO YOU BY THE ROYAL HONG KONG JOCKEY CLUB...

GOOD EVENING. TODAY'S WINNING TEMPERATURE WAS 29°. THERE WERE 1667 WINNERS...

FREDDY'S FORECAST

MORNING FOG	17-1
PARTLY CLOUDY	5-2
FINE ASIDE FROM SOME MIST	6-1
SIGNAL 8	55-1

TIP SI

(n.) Tip: small change left in appreciation — of the threat to your safety if a tip *isn't* left!

TO SUE GWOON

(n.) Public library: literally means "colouring book room"; and if you don't understand why, pick up any book in the library and feast your eyes on the pallette of ink, pencil, blood, tea and vomit on any page that hasn't already been torn out or cut to shreds!

WOW!! HOW MANY PAGES ARE IN THAT BOOK?

ABOUT HALF!

R-R-RRIP!!

113

TUNG LOH WAAN

(n.) Causeway Bay : enclave on Hong Kong island which remains under Japanese control 40 years after the surrender.

WAAN JAI

(n.) Wanchai: home of the legendary Suzie Wong... though nowadays she reportedly lives in Repulse Bay, off her royalties from the book and movie.

WOO JIU

(n.) Passport. Not to be confused with a so-called "Hong Kong British Passport", which is more useful as a flyswatter than a travel document.

THE EXCITING NEW **BN(O) PASSPORT!**

LOOKS ALMOST LIKE THE REAL THING!!

NEW BRIGHTER COLOUR PREVENTS MISTAKING IT FOR A REAL PASSPORT!

MR. CITIZEN, 3rd CLASS

BRITISH PASSPORT

GET OUT & STAY OUT

AN IDEAL — PAPERWEIGHT TABLE LEG PROP DOOR STOP COASTER

THE BEARER IS A BRITISH NATIONAL (OVERSEAS...and better damn well stay there!)

"BEARER HAS THE RIGHT OF ABODE GOD KNOWS WHERE...AS LONG AS IT'S NOWHERE NEAR THE BRITISH ISLES!"

GUARANTEED TO GET A BIG LAUGH FROM NORMALLY DOUR-FACED IMMIGRATION OFFICERS IN THE UNITED KINGDOM AND OTHER COUNTRIES!

WOO LUNG

(n.) Oolong tea; also means "muddle-headed fool". The former is not normally found in Hong Kong restaurants; the latter too often is.

WAITER, I ORDERED RICE!

JUST MINUTE.

WAITER, WILL YOU PLEASE BRING MY RICE!?

JUST MINUTE.

WHERE THE *!@✪!✄# IS MY RICE ALREADY?!!

JUST MINUTE.

WHAT'S THIS?

YOU ORDER THREE TIMES RICE!

YAN GUNG

(n.) Salary; also means artificial, as in the division in pay scale between expatriate and local staff in most offices.

IT'S UNFAIR! TO DO THE SAME JOB, YOU GET FIVE TIMES AS MUCH AS YOU NEED, WHILE I STRUGGLE WITH BARELY ANY MEANS OF SUPPORT!

WHO SAID SALARY? I'M TALKING ABOUT MY NOSE NOT SUPPORTING MY GLASSES!!

BUT I THOUGHT YOU MAKE A DECENT SALARY!

(APOLOGIES TO TIM HAMLETT!)

一九九七年

YAT GAU GAU CHAT NIN

(n.) 1997: the year Hong Kong reverts to its prior owners ... the Ching dynasty.

HE SAYS HE'S THE RIGHTFUL HEIR TO THE THRONE. HE WANTS THE DEED TO THE TERRITORY!

GOVERNOR

YAT LOK

(n.) Sunset: time of day when brilliant colours fill the sky... though in Hong Kong this isn't from the sun going down, but from the neon lights going on.

DADDY, WHAT'S A "SUNSET"?

YAU HAAK

(n.) Tourist : person who spends a fortune to fly to Hong Kong and thousands a night for a hotel, then runs around for 3 days of his time, worth US$40 an hour back home, to be overcharged three hundred bucks on a Walkman.

THE GUY IN THAT SHOP WANTED $20,000 FOR THIS CLOCK PEN, BUT I BARGAINED HIM DOWN TO $1500!

WOW, THE MONEY YOU SAVED PAYS FOR THE TRIP!

WATCHES
CLOCKS
CLOCK-PENS
$8

YI

(n.) Chair; not to be confused with YI (耳), "ear", although both are often on the receiving end of a lot of hot air.

YI YUEN

(n.) Hospital: place where you could die waiting, trying to be patient trying to be a patient.

EXCUSE ME, I'VE BEEN WAITING **FOUR** HOURS WITH SEVERE CRAMPS, A GASH IN MY NECK, A FEVER OF 42° AND A BROKEN LEG!! WHEN DO I GET TO SEE A DOCTOR???

DOCTORS VERY BUSY. YOU WAIT, OK?

YOU LOST! YOU SEE A PATIENT!

AWW, JUST ONE MORE ROUND!

YING GWOK

(n.) Britain: remote island kingdom whose inhabitants conceitedly think that anyone would want to move there before or after 1997.

IT'S BEEN LOVELY HAVING YOU AS SUBJECTS, BUT I'M SORRY, WE CAN'T HAVE YOU PEOPLE CROWDING UP OUR COUNTRY AFTER 1997!

YOU MUST BE KIDDING! TEN PERCENT UNEMPLOYMENT? RAMPANT STRIKES? RACE RIOTS? FOOTBALL HOOLIGANISM? PUNKS? THE NATIONAL FRONT? THE I.R.A.? A DYING ECONOMY, DECAYING CITIES, DECLINING MORALS? ...AND THE DREARY FOOD! YOU'D HAVE TO BE OUT OF YOUR MIND TO WANT TO LIVE IN SUCH A PLACE!!

HMM...YOU'VE GOT A POINT. DO YOU THINK IT WOULD BE HARD FOR ME TO GET A HONG KONG I.D. CARD?

YING MAN

(n.) English: once the living language of Shakespeare; now being bludgeoned to death by Japanese garment manufacturers.

YING NUI WONG

(n.) The Queen: foreigner whose face adorns Hong Kong stamps, coins, and government office walls. Though if we must have a non-resident gwaipoh for this purpose, wouldn't Christie Brinkley in a bathing suit be more attractive?

STAMPS & REGISTRATION

I'LL TAKE 20 BATHING SUITS, 12 SHORT SHORTS, 6 TOWEL WRAPS, AND A COUPLE OF EVENING GOWNS!!

LOCAL AND SLOWBOAT

AIRM

YING WONG DO

(n.) King's Road. After 1997 this will be renamed The Glorious Victory Of The Bold People's Liberation Army Martyrs Over The Heinous Running Dog Lackeys Of The Traitorous Gang Of Four Rascals Boulevard.

127

YIU YIN

(n.) Rumour: the difference between rumour and fact is the latter is rarely believable enough to be taken seriously by Hong Kong people.

YUE CHI

(n.) Shark fin soup: item placed on menus to scare the wits out of westerners.

SORRY, SIR — I THINK IT NOT COOKED LONG ENOUGH! MAYBE YOU TRY ANOTHER DISH, OK?

YUET GWONG

(n.) The moon: scientists say it's a bleak, sterile, colourless environment. In that case, it must look a lot like Discovery Bay!

WORD INDEX

索引

EXPRESSIONS